AZTECS
THE FALL OF THE
AZTEC CAPITAL

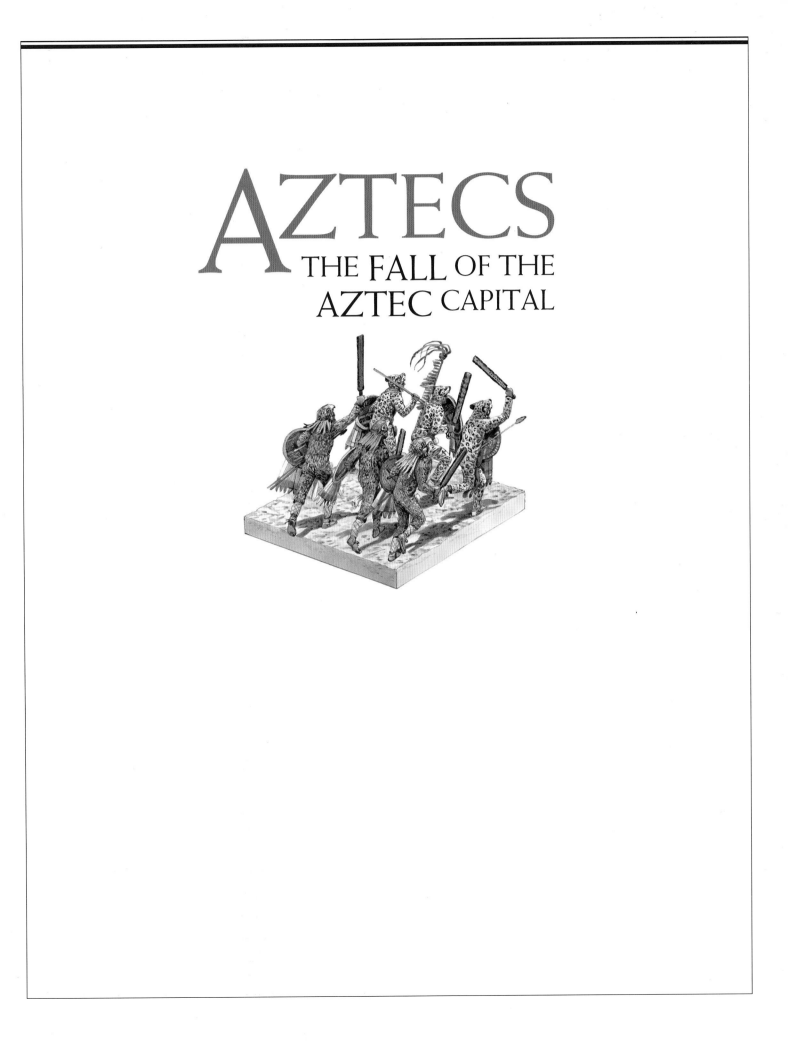

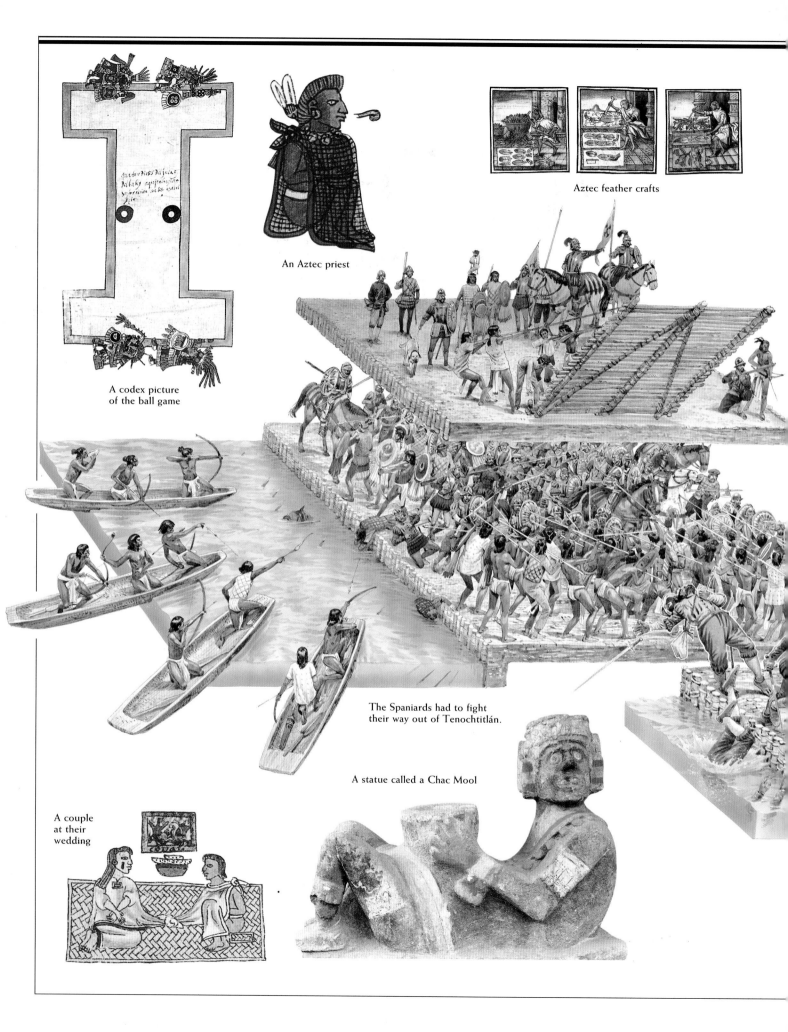

A codex picture
of the ball game

An Aztec priest

Aztec feather crafts

The Spaniards had to fight
their way out of Tenochtitlán.

A statue called a Chac Mool

A couple
at their
wedding

AZTECS
THE FALL OF THE AZTEC CAPITAL

Written by
RICHARD PLATT

Illustrated by
PETER DENNIS

A DK PUBLISHING BOOK
www.dk.com

A DK PUBLISHING BOOK
www.dk.com

Project Editor Susan Malyan
Art Editor Sarah Ponder
Senior Editor Scarlett O'Hara
Senior Art Editor Vicky Wharton
Senior Managing Editor Linda Martin
Senior Managing Art Editor Julia Harris
US Editor Lilan Patri
DTP Designer Andrew O'Brien
Picture Research Christine Rista
Jacket Designer Andrew Nash
Production Kate Oliver
Consultant Dr. Anne Millard

First American Edition, 1999

2 4 6 8 10 9 7 5 3

Published in the United States by DK Publishing, Inc.
95 Madison Avenue, New York, New York 10016

Published in Great Britain by Dorling Kindersley Limited.

Library of Congress Cataloging-in-Publication Data

Platt, Richard.
    Aztecs / by Richard Platt. -- 1st American ed.
    p. cm. -- (DK discoveries)
  Summary: A brief history of the Aztec Indians including their
way of life, religion, and rulers.
  ISBN 0-7894-3957-3
  1. Aztecs--History--Juvenile literature. 2. Aztecs--Social life
and customs--Juvenile literature. [1. Aztecs- 2. Indians of
Mexico.] I. Title. II. Series.
  F1219.73 .P53 1999
  972--dc21
                                                      99-12002
                                                      CIP

Reproduced by Colourscan, Singapore
Printed and bound by L.E.G.O., Italy

Additional illustrations by David Ashby

Contents

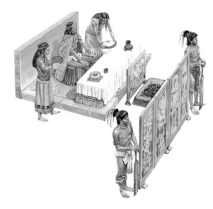

Two worlds meet

THE AZTEC EMPEROR, MOCTEZUMA, ruled the richest land in the Americas. The Spanish adventurer, Hernán Cortés, led a band of soldiers from Europe. Their meeting in 1519 led to one of the most dramatic conflicts in history.

Aztec warrior, wearing tough armor of cotton and feathers.

Like all the Aztecs, Moctezuma believed the world would end if he did not offer his gods human blood and hearts.

Spanish soldier with metal weapons and armor.

Exchanging gifts brought the two leaders together. But religion and greed would soon drive them apart.

Codex illustration of the meeting of Cortés and Moctezuma, from the book *History of the Indies of New Spain* by Diego Durán, 1579.

THE CHARACTERS

MOCTEZUMA WAS EXPECTING THE Spaniards, because mysterious omens had warned him of bad things to come. When the Spanish fleet arrived, his spies brought him the news from the coast. "We saw upon the sea some very large houses, which moved like the canoes we use to travel by water," they said. This alarmed the emperor. His priests cursed the Spaniards with magic spells, but this did not make them turn back. Believing that the strange ships had brought gods to Mexico, Moctezuma sent them gifts, and waited.

SAHAGÚN AT WORK
This Spanish monk recorded the accounts of Aztecs who had witnessed the conquest.

Bernadino de Sahagún

THE WRITERS
Bernadino de Sahagún and Francisco Lopez de Gomara were Spaniards who wrote accounts of the historic events in Mexico during and after the Spanish conquest.

THE SOLDIERS
Five hundred Spanish soldiers sailed to Mexico from Cuba. Many had sold their farms to buy weapons, armor, and horses. They were lured by stories of gold, and by the promise of land if the expedition succeeded.

Spanish soldiers

Doña Marina

THE CAPTAIN
Pedro de Alvarado was one of Cortés's 10 captains. Cortés selected Alvarado because he had traveled on an earlier expedition to Mexico.

Pedro de Alvarado

THE TRANSLATOR
The Tabascan people gave Cortés a slave girl, named Doña Marina, who already spoke several local languages. She learned Spanish and became Cortés's translator.

THE EYEWITNESS
Bernal Díaz was a 26-year-old soldier who fought in Cortés's army. He later wrote a vivid account of the things he had seen, called *The Conquest of New Spain*. Parts of it are quoted in this book.

Bernal Díaz

Hernán Cortés

Spanish priests

THE LEADER
Hernán Cortés was raised in Spain and studied law in Salamanca. At the age of 19, he sailed to the Caribbean, where he became a farmer on the island of Hispaniola. In 1519 the governor of Cuba appointed him leader of an expedition to Mexico.

THE PRIESTS
Several Christian priests traveled with the expedition. They believed that it was their mission to convert the Mexicans to Christianity.

Aztec soldiers

THE WARRIORS

Aztec soldiers had only bows, slings, spears, and stone-edged swords to defend themselves. Nevertheless, their bravery and ingenuity made them a frightening and unpredictable foe.

EYEWITNESS
"The great Montezuma was about forty years old, of good height... He had a short black beard, well shaped and thin."

Bernal Díaz, from his book *The Conquest of New Spain*, 1560s

THE EMPEROR

Emperor Moctezuma II (sometimes spelled "Montezuma") came to the Aztec throne in 1502. He had an army a thousand times bigger than that of Cortés. Moctezuma was a superstitious man, and his trust in astrologers was to prove fatal in his dealings with the Spanish.

THE AZTEC'S ALLIES

On their own, the Aztecs could not have controlled Mexico. But they had the support of two neighboring cities, Texcoco and Tlacopan. Together, this "Triple Alliance" seemed unbeatable.

King of Tlacopan

King of Texcoco

Aztec priests

AZTEC PRIESTS

Aztec people were deeply religious. Their priests led elaborate rituals and human sacrifices which they believed their gods demanded.

Emperor Cuauhtémoc

THE LAST RULER

After Moctezuma's death in 1520, his son-in-law, Cuauhtémoc, became emperor. Cuauhtémoc was determined to resist the Spaniards even if every Aztec died fighting against them.

Aztec scribes

THE SCRIBES

Aztec scribes kept religious, historical, and government records written in signs and pictures. Later they taught Spanish priests to interpret the books they had created. This preserved a record of Aztec culture.

Emperor Moctezuma II

The Aztecs and modern Mexico
Today's Mexicans are proud of their Aztec past. The national flag shows the legendary eagle, cactus, and snake emblem, and more than a million people still speak Náhuatl, the Aztec language.

Homeland in the hills
The Aztecs' home was sandwiched between two mountain ranges in Mexico's central valley. The region has a pleasant spring-like climate; it is rarely very hot or cold. Crops grow well in the fertile soil, but there is little flat land for farming. Forests cover the slopes above the valley.

WHO WERE THE AZTECS?

IN THE MIDDLE OF MEXICO LAY A fertile valley. At its center was a lake. On an island in the lake, the Mexica tribe founded a city in 1325. They were one of seven tribes of Aztec people who had wandered into the valley from the north. As the last to arrive, the Mexica got the worst land. But they made the most of it. Their city, Tenochtitlán, thrived. In 1428 they made an alliance with two nearby cities, Texcoco and Tlacopan. By the 16th century, this "Triple Alliance" controlled a kingdom of four million people. The Aztecs had become the most powerful people in Mexico.

GAZE OF AN AZTEC
Sculptures and drawings show that Aztec people looked very like their descendants, the Náhua Indians of modern Mexico. This is hardly surprising: the Aztecs outnumbered their Spanish conquerors, and marriage between the two groups soon diluted Spanish blood. Most of today's Mexicans have some Aztec ancestry.

Tarascan people threatened the Aztecs from the west.

TLACOPAN
TEXCOCO
TENOCHTITLÁN
M E X I C O

Gulf of Mexico

Pacific Ocean

This region lies on the thin bridge of land that joins North and South America.

The Aztecs could never conquer this area, controlled by the Tlaxcalan people.

THE EMPIRE GROWS
The warlike Mexica fought to defend their land and expand their empire. Forming the Triple Alliance added to their military power, and by 1519 the allies had conquered much of ancient Mexico. With each new conquest more wealth flowed to Tenochtitlán.

■ The Aztec empire in 1440

■ Extra land conquered by 1481

□ The empire in 1519, when the Spanish arrived

This codex picture illustrates the founding of Tenochtitlán.

The crossed blue lines represent the lake waters.

THE AZTECS' JOURNEY

Ancient legends tell how the Aztecs migrated from their homeland, Aztlán. The Mexica tribe was traveling near Lake Texcoco when the god Huitzilopochtli appeared to the priests in a vision. He told them to settle where they saw an eagle in a cactus eating a snake. Sure enough, they saw this strange sight on an island in the lake and founded a city there. They called it the "place of the cactus fruit," or Tenochtitlán.

Stone "blades" made the Aztecs' wooden swords razor-sharp.

Knife made of obsidian, a glass formed when lava cools.

The Toltecs

BEFORE THE AZTECS ARRIVED in Mexico's central valley, the area had been controlled by many other peoples. One group was the Toltec, whose capital city was at Tula. The Aztecs admired Toltec culture and adopted many of the Toltec gods and customs.

The raised arms would have supported an altar or a shrine.

Warrior sculpture
This Toltec figure represents a warrior in his armor. The Toltecs were a warlike people, and the Aztecs learned from them how to rule Mexico by force.

WARRIOR GOD OF THE SUN
The Aztecs believed that the sun would not rise unless they offered human hearts to its god, Huitzilopochtli.

THE AZTEC GODS

The Aztecs had about 1,600 gods – one for every aspect of their lives. They worshiped them at home shrines and also in elaborate public rituals, led by priests. The ceremonies involved dance and drama in fantastic costumes, as well as bloody human sacrifices.

CONSTANT WARFARE

Warfare was absolutely vital to Aztec society and culture. Constant wars supplied prisoners for the human sacrifices demanded by the Aztec religion. The empire's powerful army crushed any resistance to Aztec rule, and professional soldiers formed a privileged upper class.

FARMING

To feed the growing population, Aztec farmers cultivated every patch of level land. They created fields on terraces (steps) cut into the hillsides, and planted crops on land reclaimed from the lake. Aztec farming methods were more advanced than those in use in Spain.

Codices

AZTEC SCRIBES used a form of picture writing, rather like a modern comic. Much of what we know about Aztec life comes from their work, bound in books called codices. Because codices illustrated the Aztec religion, the Spaniards destroyed many of them.

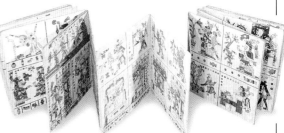

History unfolds
Unlike a book, a codex does not have a spine. Instead, the leather and bark-paper pages are hinged at both sides, like folding screens.

THE SPANIARDS ARRIVE

THE TALL, BEARDED STRANGERS arrived by sea in the Aztec year one-reed. They landed on a distant coast, but messengers brought the news quickly to the Aztec emperor, Moctezuma. He believed that the strangers were gods; in fact, they were a Spanish expedition from the island of Cuba. Their leader was Hernán Cortés. The Spaniards behaved peacefully until the people of Tabasco tried to make them leave. Then the Spaniards fought back. Armed with powerful weapons that were new to Mexico, 500 Spaniards defeated 12,000 Tabascans. From the Tabascans, the Spaniards learned that Moctezuma's kingdom was the source of the gold they were seeking.

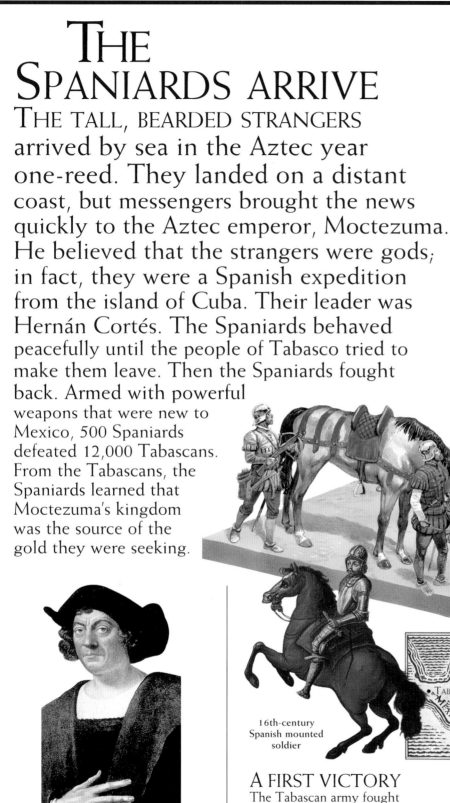

CLAIMING THE LAND

When the Spaniards landed in the Tabasco region, they quickly occupied the small coastal town of Potochán. There Cortés claimed the country for the Spanish king.

The Tabascans gave Cortés a slave, Doña Marina, who translated for him.

16th-century Spanish mounted soldier

Christopher Columbus
The Italian-born navigator Christopher Columbus sailed from Spain to the Caribbean in 1492. Over the next 25 years the Spanish settled the larger Caribbean islands, such as Cuba and Hispaniola. Stories of gold lured Spanish adventurers like Cortés to explore the mainland of Mexico.

A FIRST VICTORY

The Tabascan army fought bravely, but the Spaniards were able to defeat them because they had better weapons and tactics (methods of fighting). Horses were unknown in Mexico, and the Tabascans thought that each horse and its rider was one single, supernatural creature.

THE ROUTE TO MEXICO

Cortés and his soldiers had crossed the Atlantic years earlier. They had been living in Spanish settlements on the islands of Cuba and Hispaniola (now Haiti and the Dominican Republic). The voyage to the mainland took only four days.

Giant cottonwood (kapok) tree

> " "Many came also to gape at the strange men, now so famous, and at their attire, arms and horses, and they said 'These men are gods!' "

Francisco Lopez de Gomara, from his book *The History of the Conquest of Mexico*, 1552

Cortés made three sword cuts in a tree in the center of the town to claim the land for Spain.

NO TURNING BACK

Moctezuma's lavish gifts made Cortés even more determined to meet the emperor. Not all his men agreed – some planned to steal a ship and return to Cuba. Cortés had them executed. Then he ordered the secret sinking of his ships, so that nobody could turn back!

GIFTS FROM MOCTEZUMA

GOLD AND SILVER
Among Moctezuma's gifts was a cartwheel-sized golden sun disk and a bigger silver moon.

From Tabasco, the Spaniards sailed 250 miles (400 km) west and anchored. Three days later, at Easter 1519, a group of Aztec officials arrived, bringing gold and other gifts from Moctezuma. Cortés sent them back with cheap trinkets and a request that he might visit the emperor. The messengers reappeared a week later, with more astonishing gifts. They also brought bad news – the emperor refused to meet the Spaniards.

SKETCHING THE STRANGERS
Aztec artists drew pictures of the Spanish and their ships and horses to take back to Moctezuma.

The Aztecs needed 100 porters to carry all the gifts.

The march inland
The Spanish troops were outraged when they discovered that Cortés had destroyed their only means of escape. But there was nothing they could do. So when Cortés set off on August 16 in search of Moctezuma, his troops had no choice but to follow him.

Spanish weapons

TRAINING, DISCIPLINE, AND FIGHTING SKILLS helped the Spanish soldiers defeat much larger Mexican armies. Their superior weapons also gave them an advantage: they had cannons, muskets (small guns like rifles), crossbows, and metal armor.

Armor
Spanish soldiers wore a metal cuirass (chest and back plates) and helmet. This gave them plenty of protection against the darts, slingshot stones, and arrows fired by their Mexican enemies.

16th-century Spanish cannon

Cannon
The cannons probably were not very effective weapons, but they produced a lot of flame and noise when fired. Cortés used them to frighten the Mexicans.

Spanish soldier's helmet

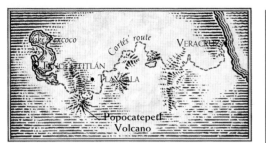

THE MARCH AND THE MEETING

FROM A SNOWY MOUNTAIN PASS, THE Spanish soldiers got their first glimpse of Tenochtitlán. Far below, the island city glittered like a jewel in the brilliant blue waters of Lake Texcoco. Four days later, on November 8, 1519, they stood on its banks. Crowds of people from the Aztec capital packed the causeway that linked it to the shore. They were curious to see if the tall foreigners in metal clothes really were gods, as they had been told. Thousands more Aztecs watched from canoes on the lake. With drums beating and flags flying, Cortés led his men to meet the Aztec emperor.

The grueling march
To reach the Aztec capital, Cortés marched his soldiers more than 400 miles (650 km) inland. They scaled two mountain ranges and crossed a plain where the water was too stagnant to drink. Native people threatened to kill them and eat their flesh with chilies. The soldiers begged Cortés to turn back. He refused, and after 12 weeks brought his little army to the gates of Tenochtitlán.

Scorched by a volcano
After resting in a nearby town, one of the Spanish captains and two of his men climbed to the top of the volcano Popocatepetl ("smoking mountain"). From the rim of the crater they could see Tenochtitlán in the distance. It was a dangerous prank – the volcano erupted, spraying rocks and hot ash all around the soldiers.

RIDING IN
The Spaniards advanced in formation, as if riding into battle.

AT THE HEAD
Cortés rode until Moctezuma approached.

Savage war dog

Tlaxcalan warriors

Bernal Díaz

Doña Marina

FOES BECOME ALLIES
Behind the Spaniards marched hundreds of warriors from Tlaxcala. The Tlaxcalans were traditional enemies of the Aztecs. Cortés defeated the Tlaxcalans and then recruited them as allies against the Aztecs.

The white heron was a Tlaxcalan emblem.

THE SPANIARDS
To the Aztecs, the Spanish soldiers seemed to possess superhuman powers. They carried magical weapons that roared and belched fire (guns). Some rode animals (horses) that had never been seen before in Mexico. And their shiny metal armor reflected the sunlight as easily as it had repelled deadly Indian arrows.

Gods or conquerors?

Wooden mask inlaid
with turquoise

MOCTEZUMA WELCOMED CORTÉS because he believed the Spaniard was the god Quetzalcóatl. According to legend, Quetzalcóatl had sailed east to join the sun god, warning that he would return. When strangers arrived from the east, Aztec elders agreed that their leader must be the returning god.

Serpent god with a human face
The Aztecs believed Quetzalcóatl could take many forms, including that of a bearded man. This wooden mask represents the god.

The god was named after the long-feathered quetzal bird.

"This is what our kings and those who ruled this city told us: that you would come to assume your rightful place... Welcome to your kingdom, lords!"

Moctezuma on first meeting Cortés, from Bernadino de Sahagún's book *A General History of the Things of New Spain,* 1580

THE AZTECS WELCOME THE SPANIARDS

As the Spaniards advanced along the causeway, Moctezuma came to welcome them to Tenochtitlán. He walked beneath a canopy of brilliant green feathers, and gold and precious stones decorated his clothes. Aztec noblemen spread their cloaks where he would walk. No one dared even look at the emperor.

CANOPY OF FEATHERS
The canopy was embroidered with gold and silver thread and bordered with pearls and turquoise stones.

AZTEC NOBLES
The brilliant colors of their cloaks showed the nobles' importance.

Many more Aztecs watched from canoes.

MESSAGE OF PEACE
Doña Marina translated as Cortés promised not to harm Moctezuma or Mexico.

THE MEETING

"Is it really you? Are you truly Moctezuma?" asked Cortés. After warm greetings, he hung colored glass beads around the emperor's neck. In exchange, Moctezuma gave him a necklace of gold crabs. Then the emperor turned back to the city. The Spaniards followed, warily. Were they walking into a trap?

The causeway was eight paces wide.

RESPECT FOR THE EMPEROR
The Aztec princes stared at the ground as a sign of respect.

THE CITY ON THE LAKE

AFTER THE GREETING ON THE CAUSEWAY, Moctezuma led his guests into an extraordinary city. Home to 200,000 people, Tenochtitlán was bigger than Spain's finest city, Seville. But it wasn't just its size that impressed the visitors. For Tenochtitlán was also beautiful, prosperous, and spotlessly clean. Great pyramids towered over the sacred center, which was surrounded by glittering palaces and vast markets selling a bewildering variety of food and luxuries. Aqueducts channeled spring water to bubbling public fountains. Tenochtitlán's splendor dazzled the Spanish guests, and they were eager to explore the city.

EYEWITNESS

"With such wonderful sights to gaze on we did not know what to say, or if this was real that we saw before our eyes."

Bernal Díaz, from his book *The Conquest of New Spain*, 1560s

LIVING LIKE GODS

Following Moctezuma's officials, the Spaniards walked to a palace next to the central square. The emperor was waiting to welcome them. He showed Cortés and his officers to fine rooms decorated with flowers, and servants brought them a delicious meal. While they stayed in the city, they would be treated like gods.

Palace courtyard

SACRED CENTER

In the center of Tenochtitlán was a walled square. Here, in temples on top of the high pyramids, Aztec holy men honored their gods with colorful ceremonies and human sacrifices. Cortés said the temples "stank of blood."

Map of Tenochtitlán
Cortés sketched a map of Tenochtitlán, and sent it to the Spanish king, Charles V. This print of the map, published in 1524, shows the causeways, central square, and houses, but not the green fields of reclaimed land that ringed the city.

INSIDE THE PALACE

The palace was built in Aztec style, with few windows and little furniture. Nevertheless, it impressed the Spaniards because most of the houses they had seen since arriving in Mexico were simple huts.

The city had a spectacular setting among mountains.

Today's city center
The siege of Tenochtitlán destroyed much of this beautiful and civilized city. Afterward, the Spaniards flattened the remainder and built what is now Mexico City on top of the ruins. The vast Zócalo Square in today's city stands roughly on the site of Tenochtitlán's sacred center. The ruins of the great pyramid lie behind the twin towers of the cathedral.

TWIN TEMPLES
On top of the great pyramid were two temples dedicated to the gods Huitzilopochtli and Tlaloc.

LAKE AND LAND
Clever engineering had turned the swampy city site into useful land. A 10-mile (16-km) long dam divided the lake and stopped salty streams from spoiling its water. Aqueducts (water bridges) brought fresh water from nearby hills. Around the city, farmers cultivated *chinampas*, raised fields made of lake-bed mud.

MARKETS
There was a small market close to the Spaniards' lodgings. They also visited a much larger one in the northern part of the city.

Selling fabric

Selling turkeys

Players struck the ball without using their hands.

Playing the ballgame

Doña Marina

Cortés

Selling fruit and vegetables

A codex picture of the ball court

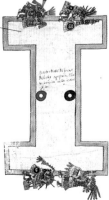

THE BALL COURT
Near the great pyramid was an I-shaped ball court. Here, teams of players, dressed in specially padded clothing, competed to knock a rubber ball through two stone rings. Gamblers bet on who would win, but the ballgame was much more than a sport. It was also a religious ritual in which the ball represented the sun, and the outcome of the game foretold the future.

VISITING THE MARKETS
After four days in Tenochtitlán, Cortés and his officers went sightseeing. They visited a huge market, selling gold and silver, slaves, cloth, chocolate, rope, animal skins, pottery, timber, and more. One soldier, Bernal Díaz, wrote, "We were astounded at the number of people and the quantity of merchandise it contained." There were even market officials to sort out disputes between traders and customers.

this city. They were surrounded and outnumbered. Escape would be impossible. One word from the emperor, and thousands of Aztec soldiers could slaughter them.

Cortés and his men hatched a plan – they would seize Moctezuma. Then, if the Aztecs attacked, they would kill the emperor. Amazingly, the daring scheme worked. With Moctezuma as their hostage, the Spaniards felt safe. But then things began to go wrong.

The governor of Cuba had realized that Cortés was no longer following his orders, so he sent a powerful army to arrest him. With 100 trusted soldiers, Cortés marched to the coast to meet them. He won an easy victory, but as he prepared to return, he got more bad news. The Aztecs had attacked the soldiers he had left behind. Now they were besieged in their palace fortress.

MOCTEZUMA SPEAKS
Spanish soldiers tried to guard Moctezuma from the stones thrown at him from the crowd.

GODS' FEAST
The Aztecs were celebrating the feast days of the gods Huitzilopochtli and Tezcatlipoca.

The Aztecs were trapped in the sacred precinct.

Cortés

Alvarado

TELL ME WHY
On his return, Cortés demanded an explanation. Alvarado said he suspected the Aztecs were going to try to free Moctezuma after the festival.

UNDER SIEGE

May 1520

The Aztecs were quick to avenge the massacre. They cut off supplies of food to the Spaniards and attacked the palace where they were holding Moctezuma. Cortés returned, but the following day the siege began again. Wave after wave of Aztec warriors charged at the palace. The Spaniards drove them back with muskets and cannons.

With only simple weapons, the Aztecs almost defeated the better-armed Spaniards.

MASSACRE AT THE FESTIVAL

Soon after Moctezuma was captured, Cortés left for the coast. His captain, Pedro de Alvarado, gave permission for the Aztecs to celebrate one of their many festivals. As the unarmed worshipers danced and sang, the Spaniards surrounded them and suddenly attacked. They murdered hundreds of Aztecs.

THE RETREAT FROM THE CITY

SOON AFTER THE SPANIARDS ARRIVED IN the city of Tenochtitlán, they made a spectacular discovery. They had noticed a section of fresh plaster on the wall of the palace. Demolishing the wall revealed Moctezuma's treasure house. Cortés could hardly believe his eyes. The whole room was piled high with gold jewelry, gold blocks, and gold plates! Despite this remarkable find, the Spaniards were still uneasy. They knew they were not truly welcome in

THE HIDDEN DOOR

A Spanish carpenter noticed a freshly plastered section of wall in the palace where they were staying. He guessed it hid a bricked-up doorway. "Open it!" ordered Cortés.

BREAKING IN
It did not take very long to reopen the bricked-up door.

Cortés

Nov 1519

THE TREASURE HOUSE

Cortés was the first to step into the treasure house and gaze in astonishment at the riches. He ordered his men not to touch the treasures, and later had the door resealed – but not before every Spanish soldier knew of the discovery.

EYEWITNESS
"What's the use of talking? Either take him or knife him. If we don't, we're dead men."

Said by Velásquez, one of Cortés's captains, from Bernal Díaz's book

Doña Marina   Cortés

The captains were secretly armed.

CAPTURED!

Cortés went to the emperor's palace with several officers and demanded that Moctezuma surrender. As an excuse, Cortés claimed that the emperor had ordered an attack on Spanish forces at the coast. Moctezuma argued at first, but then agreed to the humiliating arrest.

Making Aztec gold sculptures

TO CREATE SCULPTURES AND JEWELRY, Aztec goldsmiths used the lost-wax process. With this method, they could make countless copies of intricate designs, without losing any of the fine detail.

1 A sculptor carved a fine mold. This was the original that would be copied.

2 Wax was brushed on the mold. Then it was covered in plaster and warmed.

3 The hot wax flowed out. Melted gold was poured into the space left behind.

This Mixtec mask is a gold replica of the original mold.

The Conquest

T HE SPANISH INVADERS HAD AT LAST MET MOCTEZUMA,
but were they his guests or his prisoners? Cortés
did not wait to find out. He hatched a cunning
plan. The Spaniards might have conquered
Mexico peacefully – but instead they ended
up fighting for their lives.

The Aztecs used canoes on Lake Texcoco.

This late-18th-century painting, called *The Last Battle for Mexico*, shows the Aztecs defending Tenochtitlán against the Spanish troops.

Accident or murder?

IN TRYING TO CALM the warriors surrounding the palace, Moctezuma only angered them. The Aztecs felt their emperor had betrayed them, and pelted him with stones. Several struck Moctezuma. According to the Spaniards, the emperor died from these wounds, several days later. But Aztec accounts say that the Spaniards strangled Moctezuma and threw his body off the palace roof. Which story is true? To this day, nobody knows.

GREED FOR GOLD
Foolish Spanish soldiers filled every pocket with heavy gold.

A PLEA FOR CALM

June 29, 1520

The Aztec attacks had almost overwhelmed the Spaniards. On June 28, the Spaniards tried to escape along the causeway. Although the Aztecs drove them back, Cortés still managed to climb the Great Pyramid and set fire to the idols in the temples. The next day, Cortés took Moctezuma up onto the palace roof to try to negotiate with the Aztec soldiers. They replied with a hail of stones that knocked the emperor to the ground.

The Aztecs could have won
This codex picture, from the *Lienzo de Tlaxcala*, shows the Spaniards retreating in confusion along the causeway. The Aztecs could easily have killed all the Spaniards at this point, but this was not the Mexican way of war. Their aim was to take their Spanish enemies captive (see pages 40–41). By sparing their lives, the Aztecs gave the Spaniards a chance to escape. They seized it!

SNEAKING OUT

July 1, 1520

The Spaniards and their Tlaxcalan allies realized that they could not fight their way out of Tenochtitlán, so they decided to flee secretly at night. Cortés loaded seven horses and 80 Tlaxcalan porters with gold from the treasure house. He gave the rest of the gold to his men. They tiptoed through the silent streets and began their escape from the island city.

CONCH ALERT
The first the Spaniards knew of the ambush was the sound of the Aztec conch (shell) trumpets.

SILENT SHIPS
Under cover of darkness, the Aztecs had approached silently in their canoes and surrounded the Spaniards.

The Aztecs fought with slings, bows, and short spears.

SUDDEN ATTACK

The escaping Spaniards were soon spotted, and the Aztecs launched an ambush. Some Aztec warriors attacked from canoes, while others streamed out of Tenochtitlán. Ahead, more warriors charged at the Spaniards from the lakeside city of Tlacopan. Darts, arrows, and stones hailed down on them from all sides. The Spaniards who had already crossed the bridge spurred their horses and fled. Those on foot had to fight their way out.

SPOTTED!

The silent column of Spanish soldiers got as far as the causeway without attracting attention. As they began to cross it, some Aztec women spotted them. Their shouts alerted a watchman on the top of the Great Pyramid, and he raised the alarm.

SENTRIES
The Aztec women who spied the Spaniards were fetching water from the lake.

EYEWITNESS

"Montezuma was hit by three stones...and though they begged him to have his wounds dressed...he refused. Then quite unexpectedly we were told that he was dead."

Bernal Díaz, from his book
The Conquest of New Spain, 1560s

FORGOTTEN WEAPONS
The Spaniards made a terrible mistake when they crossed the bridge. The party that led the way did not include all the soldiers armed with crossbows and muskets.

CROSSING THE GAP

To prevent the Spaniards from escaping, the Aztecs had removed the drawbridges that spanned the gaps in the causeway. Cortés knew this, and his carpenters had built a portable bridge. They carried it to the causeway and gently lowered it into place. Cortés and his officers filed across on horseback.

ALVARADO'S LEAP

The Aztec attack destroyed the Spanish bridge, and Pedro de Alvarado was cut off from his comrades. Thrusting his lance into the lake bed, he saved himself by vaulting across the gap.

The Spanish survivors fled for their lives.

Many Spanish soldiers drowned in the lake, weighed down by the gold they were carrying.

THE NIGHT OF SORROW

As they retreated from Tenochtitlán, very few of the Spaniards escaped injury. By the time the sun rose on July 1, about two-thirds of the Spaniards and 4,000 of the Tlaxcalans had been killed. The Spaniards named the defeat *La Noche Triste* – The Night of Sorrow.

Those who escaped were mostly the experienced soldiers who had taken the least gold.

How the ships were made
The Spanish army included shipwrights and carpenters. They cut trees from the Mexican forests for wood, and boiled pine resin to seal the cracks between the planks. A thousand Indians were sent to the coast to fetch the ironwork, ropes, and sails that Cortés had salvaged from his fleet before sinking it.

CONSTRUCTION KIT
Each plank was marked to show where it fit in the ship.

THE SIEGE OF TENOCHTITLÁN

THE AZTECS HUMILIATED THE SPANIARDS when they drove them out of Tenochtitlán. Cortés lost all his guns and two-thirds of his men. But he was not defeated. The strongest and bravest Spanish soldiers had survived. New troops joined them from Cuba, bringing horses, guns, and supplies. Cortés trained more Tlaxcalan allies and built ships to fight on the lake. Then, after Christmas 1520, he led an army of 16,000 men back to Tenochtitlán. The Aztecs were ready for them. They had a new leader, Cuauhtémoc, and they were eager for a fight.

SHIPBUILDING

Cortés believed that with ships he could control Lake Texcoco and starve the Aztecs into surrender. His craftsmen cut enough lumber to build 13 ships. Then 8,000 men carried the parts 50 miles (80 km) to the lake to be reassembled.

IN CHARGE
A Spaniard named Martin López supervised the shipbuilding.

ON THE CANAL
Thousands of Tlaxcalans worked for seven weeks digging a canal from the construction site to the lake.

BRIGANTINES
The ships, called brigantines, were probably flat-bottomed so that they could sail in the shallow lake.

DEFENDING THE CITY

The Aztecs prepared for the attack they knew was coming. They built barricades of rubble and timber. They removed the bridges that spanned gaps in the causeways, and hid deadly sharp stakes underwater.

Wood from the bridges was used for barricades.

One or two planks were left for crossing but could be quickly removed.

Oars allowed the Spanish ships to chase the Aztec canoes.

EYEWITNESS
"Whenever we left some bridge or barricade unguarded...they would retake it that night, strengthen the defenses, and dig holes under the water into which we should stumble and fall."

Bernal Díaz, from his book
*The Conquest of
New Spain*, 1560s

THE SIEGE BEGINS

The battle for the city began on June 1, 1521. Cortés had split his troops into three groups and they attacked along the three main causeways that led into the city. The Aztecs fought them every step of the way.

Map of the Spanish attack

➤ Sandoval attacked from the north.

➤ Alvarado attacked from the west.

➤ Cortés attacked from the south.

War on the causeways
The Aztecs were frightening foes. They sacrificed Spanish prisoners in sight of their comrades, and rolled their heads along the causeways.

BATTLE FOR THE LAKE

Once Cortés was in control of the towns around the lakeshore, his fleet set sail. Aztec canoes soon surrounded the ships and a ferocious battle began. Spanish cannons and muskets easily sank the Aztec craft and killed their crews.

FIGHT FOR THE CENTER

The Aztecs defended their streets bravely. It took Cortés three months to reach the sacred center. The fighting was so intense that the lake water turned red with blood, and advancing Spanish soldiers had to walk on the corpses of dead Aztecs.

The Spanish destroyed every building.

Each ship was armed with several small cannons.

CANOE POWER
The Spaniards could never completely control the lake, because they had only 13 ships. There were more than 200,000 Aztec canoes.

Cortés

Cuauhtémoc

The Aztecs surrender
By August, it was clear that the Aztecs were defeated. Cuauhtémoc tried to flee in a canoe, but he was captured by the Spaniards. This scene from the Codex Lienzo de Tlaxcala shows Cuauhtémoc surrendering to Cortés.

The End of the Empire

IT WAS AN UTTERLY unbelievable victory. Two years after landing with just 500 soldiers, Hernán Cortés had defeated a vast military empire. Years before, Aztec astrologers had spotted many strange signs and omens, from which they predicted the arrival of the Spaniards. Yet even the astrologers did not foresee how completely the pale-skinned strangers would destroy their entire civilization.

> "A full two years before the Spaniards arrived, many signs and omens were seen...particularly one. It was that in the sky a tongue of fire of notable size and brightness appeared. When the people saw this flame emerge they would cry out, sensing that it was an omen of some great evil to come."
>
> Bernadino de Sahagún, from his book
> *A General History of the Things of New Spain*, 1580

The "tongue of fire" in the sky that the Aztecs took for an evil omen was actually a comet.

When an earthquake shook Mexico, Aztec wise men took it as a sign of bad things to come.

A Catholic rosary (prayer beads). The Spaniards brought a new religion to Mexico.

This scene from the Codex Florentino shows the comet in the sky over Tenochtitlán.

EYEWITNESS

"All the houses and stockades in the lake were full of heads and corpses...we could not walk without treading on the bodies and heads of dead Indians."

Bernal Díaz, from his book
The Conquest of New Spain, 1560s

AFTER THE BATTLES

WHEN THE EMPEROR CUAUHTÉMOC surrendered, fighting in Tenochtitlán soon ended. The silent, conquered city reeked of death. While the Aztecs buried the dead, the Spaniards had other things to do. They crushed rebellions in parts of Mexico that still resisted their rule, and began a desperate search for gold. It produced little. Cortés divided what he found among his men, but it was small reward for what they had suffered. His soldiers were so angry that they scrawled slogans attacking Cortés on the wall of the luxurious palace where he lived.

DEATH OF THE AZTEC LEADERS

The Spaniards tortured Cuauhtémoc and other leaders by burning their feet. When one cried out in pain, the emperor replied, "Do you think I'm lying here on a bed of roses?" Cuauhtémoc's own execution is shown in this painting.

This codex picture shows a Spanish tribute collector.

Aztec slaves were usually branded on the cheeks.

SEARCH FOR GOLD

The Spaniards looked everywhere for the treasure that they had left behind when they fled from Tenochtitlán. Gold obsessed them. But even under torture, the Aztec leaders could not tell them where most of it was hidden.

The Aztecs were forced to pay tribute in gold jewelry to their new Spanish masters.

WARRIORS MADE SLAVES

Cortés punished the Aztec soldiers who had defended their city so bravely by making them slaves. His men branded them, burning marks on their skin with red-hot irons. Some of the slaves were sent to work in the gold and silver mines. Other slaves were given to Cortés's men to reward them for their bravery in battle.

This 16th-century painting shows Aztec slaves laying the foundations for the cathedral in Mexico City.

Foundations of the cathedral

Slaves had to transport heavy loads of stone and were often worked to death.

FORCED LABOR

Unable to reward his men with gold, Cortés instead gave his officers estates and workers to farm them. The workers had to supply food, fuel, and labor for their master. A Spaniard granted an estate was supposed to protect his Aztec workers and teach them Christianity, but in practice, many workers were badly treated. The Spaniards also used Aztec slaves to build Mexico City.

Built on Aztec foundations
Although the Spaniards demolished Tenochtitlán, they could not completely destroy the Aztec buildings. When rebuilding began, resourceful Spanish masons salvaged and reused Aztec stonework. This Aztec dragon's head glowers from the doorway of a building in Mexico City.

FACT file

- 100,000 Aztecs died defending Tenochtitlán. Many more died of disease or starvation.

- If the Great Pyramid still stood, it would loom on the skyline just behind the cathedral.

- Cortés rewarded each Spanish foot soldier with the sum of just 50 pesos – enough money to buy three cows.

PYRAMID TO CATHEDRAL

Cortés had Tenochtitlán demolished, and rebuilt the city from scratch in the Spanish style. It was renamed "Mexico City." Where the sacred precinct had stood, the Spaniards built a huge square and a cathedral. The rebuilding work would have been impossible without the forced labor of the Aztecs.

Cortés's original cathedral was replaced by this much bigger one, built between 1573 and 1813.

The Plaza Mayor, now known as Zócalo Square

A painting of the Mexico City cathedral by the artist Carl Nebel, from a guide to Mexico published in 1836.

CONQUERORS WITH CROSSES

AS MEXICO CITY ROSE FROM THE RUINS of Tenochtitlán, the Spaniards started to expand their territory in Central America. The Mayan people and the inhabitants of the Pacific coast resisted the conquistadores (Spanish conquerors), but many regions welcomed them. They soon discovered, however, that they had exchanged one powerful overlord for another. Most Spaniards cared little for the welfare or traditions of the region's native peoples. They simply replaced the religion, language, laws, and customs of Mexico with those of Spain. But Cortés and his followers did not destroy the culture of the Aztecs entirely. Today the country's past lives on in many aspects of Mexican society.

> "Send me some gold, for I and my companions suffer from a disease of the heart, which can only be cured by gold."
>
> Cortés's message to Moctezuma, from the book *The History of the Conquest of Mexico* by Francisco Lopez de Gomara, 1552

RAISING CROSSES
Mexican people who became Christians often helped enthusiastically in the destruction of the old temples and the building of new Christian shrines.

BAPTISM CEREMONY
Priests welcomed converts to the Christian faith by baptizing them with water. Converts were given new, Christian names.

Building on the past
To stress that their Catholic religion was more powerful than Aztec beliefs, the Spaniards often built churches and chapels directly on top of the demolished Aztec temples. Under this church, in the town of Mitla, are the remains of a temple, possibly built by the neighboring Mixtec people.

CHRISTIANITY
In 1524, 12 Franciscan monks arrived from Spain to help spread the Christian religion. Many more followed. Eventually most Mexican people became Catholics. Besides spreading the gospel, the priests often defended Aztec people who were being exploited and ill-treated by the Spaniards. By preaching in the Náhuatl language, some priests came to understand, appreciate, and eventually write down some of the Mexican traditions.

TRUE CONVERTS?
It is hard to tell how many of the people who were baptized really gave up their traditional beliefs. Some priests suggested that in place of 1,000 gods, Aztec people who converted to Christianity now had 1,001!

A scene from the *Lienzo de Tlaxcala* codex

Coat of arms of the Spanish king, Charles V

Spanish viceroys

Lords of Tlaxcala

NEW DISEASES

In 1520, a Spanish soldier fell sick with smallpox. This European disease was unknown in Mexico, so the people had no natural resistance. The following year, smallpox killed up to half of Mexico's population. This scene from the Codex Florentino shows the suffering of smallpox victims.

GOVERNING THE COLONY

From 1535, Mexico was ruled by Spanish governors, called viceroys. The viceroys often tried to protect the native Mexicans, but settlers and corrupt officials resisted them. Eventually, only people with Spanish ancestors were allowed land, power, and justice.

The Spanish made coins, like these doubloons, from Aztec gold.

Falling population

AFTER THE CONQUEST, the population of Mexico fell very rapidly. European diseases killed millions of people; others died of starvation or ill-treatment by their Spanish masters.

Epidemics
Smallpox, measles, mumps, typhus, and tuberculosis killed huge numbers of Mexicans. There were major epidemics in 1545–6 and 1576–9.

In 1519, 25 million people lived in Mexico.

In 1538, there were 6.3 million people.

By 1580, fewer than 2 million people remained.

MEXICAN GOLD

The Spaniards melted any Aztec gold objects they could find. They sent the gold back to Spain, where it was used for coins. So much gold flooded onto the European market that it caused prices to rise.

FACT file

• The first bishop of Mexico boasted that in just five years he had destroyed 500 temples and 20,000 idols.
• The Spanish called their Mexican colony "New Spain."
• Mexico was to be ruled by the Spanish for 300 years. It did not become an independent country until 1822.

The mother talks to her child.

Rosettes show the baby's age in days.

A midwife takes the child to be washed.

Spanish text

Picture of a mother caring for her four-day old baby, from the Codex Mendoza

RECORDS OF AZTEC LIFE

To try to understand and convert the Aztecs, some Spanish priests asked them to record details of their life in codex form. The priests added notes in Spanish to explain the pictures.

Mexican girls at their first communion

The Spanish influence lives on
Today, Spanish is still the main language in Mexico. The Spaniards also succeeded in their aim of bringing Christianity to Mexico – 95 percent of today's Mexicans are Catholics. Nevertheless, a few people still practice traditional religions.

The Aztec Way of Life

USING THEIR MILITARY STRENGTH, THE AZTECS created a well-ordered world. Wealthy nobles governed the empire, while hard-working farmers fed it and fought for it. Priests in bloodstained robes prayed for it. But, at the empire's edges, conquered peoples had to pay taxes to a distant emperor, whom they hated.

A backstrap loom, used by Aztec women for weaving cloth.

An Aztec feather worker

A fresco called The Great City of Tenochtitlán painted by the modern Mexican artist, Diego Rivera, in 1945.

Towering pyramid-temples marked the religious heart of the city and empire.

Merchants and tax collectors traveled along the roads, bringing riches back to Tenochtitlán.

AZTEC SOCIETY

A WALK DOWN A BUSY TENOCHTITLÁN STREET would have revealed how Aztec society worked. Dressed in plain, cheap clothes, poor farmers and craft workers would have made up most of the crowd. The few wealthy, noble Aztecs would have been easy to spot. They wore brilliant, feathered costumes, and everyone stood aside and bowed when they passed. These nobles had power and wealth only because their parents had enjoyed similar advantages. Other groups, such as warriors and priests, fought, worked, or studied to earn special privileges. Even among ordinary Aztecs there were differences. Some owned the land they farmed, but landless peasants and slaves had the lowest social status.

EMPEROR

With his allies in the Triple Alliance, Moctezuma II ruled the vast Aztec empire. He lived in great luxury, and had an almost god-like status.

TLATOANI
A king of a city-state, who owned all the land.

NOBLES
Between 10 and 20 percent of all Aztecs were nobles. They were entitled to wear jewelry and decorated capes, and to live in two-story houses.

In this codex picture, the god of Aztec traders carries crossroads on his back. The footprint symbol indicates a journey.

Yacatecuhtli, god of traders

Feather merchant

PRIESTS
The emperor was the chief priest. Senior priests were always nobles, but other Aztecs could study for lower ranking jobs.

QUETZALCÓATL
One of the two high priests at the Great Pyramid.

TLAMACAZTON
These "little priests" were boys training for the priesthood — not all of them succeeded.

TLENAMACAC
A "fire priest" who wielded the flint knife at temple sacrifices.

Trade and travel
Tenochtitlán's markets were full of local farmers exchanging produce for the cocoa beans and cotton capes that the Aztecs used as money. In long-distance trade, traveling merchants exported cloth, garments, herbs, dyes, blankets, and stone knives, and returned to Tenochtitlán with feathers and other luxuries.

PLUME TRADE
Aztec merchants traveled great distances to buy the feathers of parrots, macaws, and quetzals.

MERCHANTS
Pochteca (traveling merchants) had a higher status than other commoners. They supplied imported luxuries, and sometimes spied for the Aztec empire.

PEASANT FARMERS
Aztec farming families lived in communities of 10–20 households. Each family owned land where they grew crops for food and for tribute.

Porters carried the goods.

Land was passed to children when the parents died.

Only the emperor could wear turquoise green clothes.

This serpent necklace made of jade was worn by a priest.

CRAFT WORKERS

Jewelers, potters, weavers, stonemasons, and feather workers all had their own craft guilds. They worked in studios on the outskirts of the towns. These craft workers were often foreigners. The few surviving examples of their work are skilful masterpieces.

PIPILTIN
A noble who served a tecuhtli.

TECUHTLI
A high-ranking noble who had been granted some land.

These symbols represent speech, and show that the father is giving instructions to his sons.

Codex picture of a father teaching his two sons.

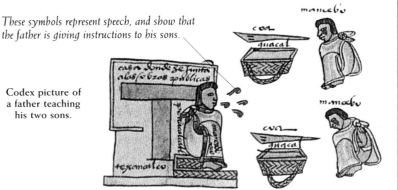

JAGUAR WARRIOR
A noble who was a member of one of the elite military orders.

OFFICER
He led the troops into battle.

WARRIORS

All boys trained in warfare at school. Those who rose to high rank won the right to dine at the royal palace, wear fine clothes, and drink alcohol.

SOLDIER
Ordinary Aztecs became soldiers when danger threatened the empire.

EDUCATION

The children of nobles or wealthy merchants could attend the *calmecac* (temple school), to become priests. Other boys attended the *telpochcalli* (house of the young men), where they learned the skills a warrior would need.

Getting drunk was a crime for anyone except old people.

LANDLESS PEASANTS

Not all Aztec commoners owned land. A *tlalmaitl* rented land from a noble, paying for it with a share of his crops.

SLAVES

The humblest of the Aztecs were the slaves, but even they had some rights. They could save money, buy houses or land, and marry free Aztecs.

War may have driven a tlalmaitl from the land he owned.

The children of slaves were born free people.

Old woman

Alcoholic drink

THE LAW

The Aztecs had a well-developed legal system: codices record punishments for 80 different crimes. Justice was swift and severe, so crime was rare. Nobles were expected to be more law-abiding than commoners.

THE EMPEROR'S GOLDEN COURT

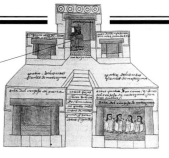

ROOM AT THE TOP
Codex pictures show the emperor on the upper floor of the palace.

IN HIS PALACE AT THE HEART OF TENOCHTITLÁN the Aztec emperor lived a life of utter luxury. A hundred wives surrounded him. He ate tasty delicacies while jugglers entertained him. Then he strolled in water gardens, where exotic birds ate from his hand. To live in this style, Moctezuma and the nobles of his court used up much of the wealth of the Aztec empire. The Mexican people had to give one-third of everything they produced in taxes and tribute to support the emperor.

Simple palace buildings
The Spaniards destroyed Tenochtitlán's palaces, so we can only guess what they looked like from descriptions and codex pictures (see above). Moctezuma's palace was on only two floors, but it covered a vast area. The many rooms were grouped around three courtyard-gardens.

PONDS AND POOLS
The sound of water echoed around the palace gardens. It splashed in cascades and fountains and filled the emperor's outdoor baths.

A servant did not dare look at the emperor.

THE GARDENS
The emperor's gardens amazed the Spaniards. Countless gardeners tended the beds of scented flowers and planted medicinal herbs. Tame birds sang in the trees. There were summerhouses where Moctezuma rested during his walks and watched performances by dancers and singers.

Everyone approaching Moctezuma went barefoot as a sign of respect.

Chili

Vanilla pods

Cocoa beans

GOLD SCREEN
Nobles sometimes kept Moctezuma company behind the screen, but they never sat at his table.

Luxurious chocolate
Moctezuma drank bitter *chocolatl*, a drink made from cocoa beans and flavored with cinnamon, vanilla, and chilies. Only nobles could afford this drink, because cocoa beans were so valuable to the Aztecs that they were used as a form of money.

DINING ALONE
Though relatives and nobles shared his crowded palace, the Aztec emperor lived apart from them. At meals he sat alone, at a table hidden from view. Beautiful women washed his hands, then served the food he had chosen from a long menu.

FACT file
- Moctezuma's servants prepared him more than 30 different dishes for each meal.
- Every day he was offered turkey, pheasant, partridge, quail, duck, venison, rabbit, and more.
- Moctezuma was served his chocolate drink in cups made of pure gold.
- While the emperor was eating, the guards in the adjoining rooms did not dare to speak.

Birds of prey

Keepers fed each bird the food it would eat in the wild.

HOUSE OF FEATHERS

Moctezuma had two huge aviaries where he kept every imaginable kind of bird. In the "House of Feathers," flamingos waded in wide ponds and colorful parrots nested. Three hundred servants fed and groomed the tame birds. When the birds were about to molt, the keepers plucked out their feathers to make clothes for the city's nobles.

NATURAL HABITATS
The ponds imitated the birds' natural habitats. There were separate pools of salt and fresh water.

AVIARY WORKERS
Cleaning the ponds, stocking them with fish, feeding, and even delousing the birds kept the workers busy.

CAGED BEASTS
The wild animals were kept in wooden cages.

AT NIGHT
The roars, howls, and cries of the animals could be heard around the city at night.

THE ZOO

In the "House of the Hunting Birds", Moctezuma also kept wild beasts in cages. Here Cortés saw lions, tigers, lynxes, and wolves. Reptiles such as crocodiles and snakes lived in big pottery jars. Keepers fed the animals on wild game, but told the Spaniards that after sacrifices, the animals ate human meat, and the snakes drank blood.

Cortés described the snakes as, "fierce and poisonous, and ugly."

Clothes for the rich

STRICT LAWS CONTROLLED how Aztec people dressed, because clothes showed the status of the people who wore them. Common people could wear only plain garments, but nobles were allowed greater choice. Their cotton clothes were decorated with feathers, furs, and gold, and dyed brilliant colors.

Noble women
Nobles dressed in bright blouses and skirts. They wore expensive jewelry and sometimes tinted their faces with light yellow makeup.

Noble men
Like the humblest workers, noble men wore a loin-cloth and cloak. However, both were elaborately embroidered, and the cloak was decorated with feathers.

Glittering gold
Fine gold jewelry suggested high status in Aztec society. Both noble men and women wore necklaces, and bracelets on their arms and legs.

Only nobles could afford shoes. Common people went barefoot.

Feather workers crafted cloaks that were warm and very beautiful.

These brilliant green plumes came from the tail of the quetzal bird.

Feathered finery
Feathered garments identified high-ranking Aztec officials and warriors. The best feather work, though, was reserved for the emperor. This tall feather crown is a reconstruction of a gift from Moctezuma to Cortés.

LIFE ON THE LAKE

WHEN THE SPANIARDS MARCHED INTO Tenochtitlán, many ordinary Aztecs watched from canoes. To these workers and farmers, the meeting on the causeway was a welcome break from a life of hard work and hunger. On small family plots they grew just enough food to feed their families. Any extra went as tribute to Moctezuma. Peasants were part-time soldiers, too. By fighting bravely in the constant wars, they won honor, extra land, and a better life.

HOME CRAFTS

An Aztec's home was a workplace, too. Farmers who had a craft skill, such as pottery, could make goods like this bowl for their own use or to sell in the gigantic city markets that had so amazed Cortés.

Grinding chilies in a bowl made a fine paste.

Chilies

STRANGE FOOD
Poor people supplemented their diet with slugs, tadpoles, flies, and worms.

Beans

Tomato

A SIMPLE DIET

Poor Aztecs ate mostly corn flour, cooked as porridge or baked into pancakes called tortillas. They also enjoyed sweet potatoes, beans, and avocados. Chilies, onions, and tomatoes added flavor. Meat was a treat, but at festivals Aztecs ate turkey washed down with *pulque* – agave juice fermented into alcohol. The lake provided food that we might find strange. Floating algae could be made into a sort of cheesecake; and the eggs of water insects were a delicacy.

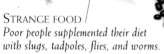

Neck of huipilli *(blouse) decorated with embroidery*

Men wore loincloths when they worked.

Corn

COOKING
This pottery disk had a rough base to transfer heat to the tortillas on top.

Tortillas

Peanuts

CHILD LABOR

"Childhood" lasted only to the age of six or seven. Older children watched their parents work and copied their tasks. The children of farmers attended the *telpochcalli* ("house of the young men"), where the boys trained as warriors.

PUNISHMENT
Parents held a naughty child over a fire stoked with chilies.

PLAIN CLOTHES

Ordinary people could not afford the brilliant garments that Cortés saw the Aztec nobles wearing. Farmers and laborers tied a plain loincloth around their waist and kept out the cold with a cape woven from coarse agave fibers. Women's clothes were equally plain – an ankle-length skirt held up by a belt. Poor women went topless, but wealthier women wore blouses.

HUMBLE HOUSES

Basic Aztec homes were single rooms of mud brick. All but the humblest, though, had a separate kitchen and bathroom. As families grew and prospered, householders added rooms, but their homes remained very simple. The only furnishings were mats for sleeping and sitting on, and small basketwork chests for possessions. A farming family's land surrounded the house, and in the *chinampa* region a nearby canal was a water supply, food source, and highway.

Girls learned craft skills from their mothers.

The family ate and slept together in one room.

WATERPROOF ROOF
A thatched roof of grass or reeds kept out the rain.

LIVING OUTDOORS
Very cold or very hot weather is rare in Mexico's central valley, so families could spend a lot of time outside.

JOBS FOR WOMEN

A few Mexican women gained independence as healers, midwives, or priestesses. Widows and older women earned respect for their wisdom and experience. But most had little real power – crafts, farming, housework, and children took up all their energy and time.

Cooking pots rested on three hearth stones.

DUG-OUT TRANSPORT
Canoes made from hollowed-out logs were the only means of transport: there were no wheeled carts, and no pack animals.

Anglers fished with nets and three-pointed spears

PREPARING DINNER
Corn was ground with a stone roller to make the flour for tortillas.

NETTING GAME
Migrating ducks and geese were an important source of protein. They were trapped in nets.

Floating gardens

FARMLAND WAS SCARCE in the area around Tenochtitlán. Farmers cut terraces in hillsides, and even farmed the lake. They created fields called *chinampas* (floating gardens), which didn't really float. They were actually reclaimed land, arranged in a grid pattern with canals between each piece.

Water level

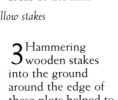

1 Lake Texcoco was gradually drying up. As the water level fell, new areas of marsh and mud appeared in shallow areas of the lake.

Raised ground is drier

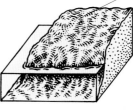

2 Farmers scooped soil from the lake bed. They piled it onto marshy areas to form rectangular plots, separated by deep water channels.

Willow stakes

3 Hammering wooden stakes into the ground around the edge of these plots helped to prevent the soil from being washed away.

Grazing turkeys

4 The stakes grew into trees that sheltered crops and livestock. Their tangled roots reinforced the banks of the *chinampas*.

WAR AND THE EMPIRE

IMAGINE A WORLD CONSTANTLY AT war, where success depended on bravery on the battlefield, and where mock battles replaced real ones whenever there was peace. This was the world in which the Aztecs lived. Valiant Aztec warriors were heroes and lived in great luxury. Their fighting skills allowed Tenochtitlán and its two allied cities to rule the whole of central Mexico. Military power made the Triple Alliance rich, and neighboring peoples poor. Success in battle also brought a constant supply of captives for sacrifices. The Aztecs believed that these bloody religious rituals would assure them of yet more victories.

> "This Indian, who was called Tzilacatzin, appeared in Otomi dress... attacking the enemy without fearing anyone, as if in a daze."
>
> Bernadino de Sahagún, from his book *A General History of the Things of New Spain*, 1580

An oak dart with a stone point

Atlatl

Aztec weapons
Using a throwing stick, called an *atlatl*, a warrior could hurl darts about 200 ft (60 m). Two new weapons – bows and broadswords – gave the Aztecs an advantage over neighboring peoples.

AZTEC WARRIORS
Every Aztec man had to do military service in the emperor's army. Apprentice warriors wore only a loincloth and war paint. They fought with bows and *atlatls*. Taking captives brought a warrior promotion, armor, better weapons, and higher status on the battlefield and at home.

NOVICE FIGHTER
An apprentice warrior had no armor and carried only basic weapons.

Lightweight basketwork shield covered in leather

Oak broadsword with edges of sharp stone

Elite Aztec warriors

The Wars of the Flowers
"Flower Wars" were small, formal battles that the Aztecs used to keep hostile neighbors at bay and take captives for sacrifice. A few troops from each side would fight at a pre-arranged time and place. By repeated victories in these battles, the Aztecs would eventually conquer the enemy.

KNIGHT IN ARMOR
Successful warriors had armor and better weapons. They wore starched, quilted-cotton armor to stop arrows and darts.

THE GOD OF WAR
Huitzilopochtli, the god of war, was one of the most important gods. The Aztecs believed that he guided their military campaigns, provided them with weapons, and guaranteed victory. In return, Huitzilopochtli demanded constant offerings of human blood and hearts.

Paying tribute

WHEN THE TRIPLE ALLIANCE conquered a region, the citizens had to pay tribute to their new rulers. Tribute was a tax, paid in possessions or in work. Collectors traveled to each village to make sure the tribute was paid. Enriched by this flow of wealth from the countryside, the alliance grew immensely powerful.

Tribute lists

Aztec scribes used tribute lists to record how much each conquered town had to pay. At the top of this list, from the Codex Mendoza, are two rows of cloaks. The symbols above them show the number required – 400 of each type.

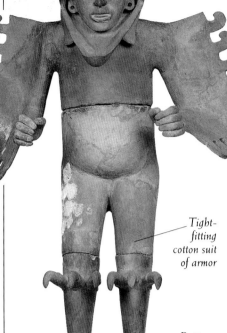

Tight-fitting cotton suit of armor

Pottery statue of an eagle warrior

Eagle warrior

Noble soldiers who took four captives joined the elite eagle or jaguar troops. They wore armor shaped like these creatures. Further captives earned promotion to an *Otomi*, or "Shorn Warrior."

MISSILE ATTACK
The battle began with a one-minute barrage of spears, arrows, and stones.

Warriors with slings could fire stones several hundred yards (meters).

An Aztec broadsword was sharp enough to cut off a horse's head with a single blow.

THE CHARGE
Elite eagle and jaguar warriors led the charge against the enemy. Experienced soldiers followed. Apprentice troops guarded the sides and rear.

SWORD FIGHT
Once the battle with swords and thrusting spears began, missiles became useless because they might hit friendly soldiers.

THE BATTLE BEGINS

Aztec battles began at dawn. Opposing troops faced each other about 55–65 yards (50–60 m) apart. Signals on trumpets and drums ordered the soldiers to advance. The frontline troops fought in an unbroken row to protect each other, and tried to break the enemy line into smaller, weaker groups.

Aztec warrior

Captive

CAPTIVES FOR SACRIFICE

Warriors captured on the battlefield were taken back to Tenochtitlán. They were kept in prison and later sacrificed to the Aztec gods. Until they were killed at the temple, they were worshiped as gods.

TAKING A CAPTIVE
Killing the enemy was not the main aim of warfare. Aztec warriors gained greater honor by taking prisoners alive. The more ferocious the prisoner, the more glory his captor won.

RELIGION AND SACRIFICE

ACROSS THE SACRED PRECINCT, a scream of agony rang out. Then a priest appeared at the top of the highest pyramid. Blood spattered his brilliantly colored feather cape. He held in his hands a still-beating human heart. Seconds later, the limp body of its owner tumbled down the side of the steep temple-pyramid. The sacred ritual was complete; the priests had offered the man's heart and blood to their gods. The warrior who had captured him in battle would soon eat parts of the corpse in a solemn religious feast. Human sacrifices like these filled the Spaniards who watched them with horror. Yet the Aztec people believed that if the rituals stopped, the crops would fail, the seasons would not change, and the sun would not rise – life itself would end.

AZTEC PRIESTS
Aztec priests lived simple lives and were not allowed to marry. Their duties did not end when the gruesome temple ceremonies finished. Each night they cut open their ears to offer some of their own blood to the gods.

Sometimes hundreds of victims were sacrificed in one day.

Blood covered the priests' robes and ran down the steps.

HUMAN SACRIFICE
The Aztecs believed that the gods had given their own blood when they created the world. Human sacrifices repaid them. Priests would stretch a captive across a stone at the top of the sacred pyramid, and rip out his heart with a flint knife. They offered the heart to the gods, and tossed the body down the pyramid steps.

STAIRWAY TO DEATH
A staircase of 113 steps led to the top of the pyramid.

The Day of the Dead
Spanish attempts to stamp out the Aztec religion were only partly successful. Today, Mexicans still celebrate the Day of the Dead. They give skull-shaped gifts and candies: a reminder of the bloody rituals that ended centuries ago.

EYEWITNESS
"They strike out the wretched Indian's chest with flint knives, and hastily tear out the palpitating heart, which, with the blood, they present to the idols."

Bernal Díaz, from his book
The Conquest of New Spain, 1560s

ROUND STONE
The lifeless bodies of the sacrificial victims fell onto this round stone, which was unearthed by archaeologists in 1978.

Idol of the god Xipe Totec

The Aztec gods

WHEN AZTEC WARRIORS defeated a town, they took the local idols as trophies, and adopted the gods as their own. This swelled the number of Aztec gods to 1,600 or more. However, only a few of the gods were honored with important yearly festivals. Huitzilopochtli, the god of war and the sun, was especially sacred in Tenochtitlán. Other gods represented the elements, plants, or ancestors.

IDOLS

Aztec people prayed to idols – statues of their gods. Many people had small pottery idols in their homes. There were much bigger idols in the temples, often decorated with gold and precious stones.

Tlaloc
This ancient god of rain and fertility was worshiped with Huitzilopochtli on the Great Pyramid.

Tezcatlipoca
Tezcatlipoca, or "smoking mirror," controlled everyone's fate and was perhaps the most powerful of all the gods.

Quetzalcóatl
A snake with the green feathered tail of the quetzal represented the nature god, Quetzalcóatl. This was also the title given to the two most important temple priests.

This bird-snake god could also take human form.

Temple of Tlaloc

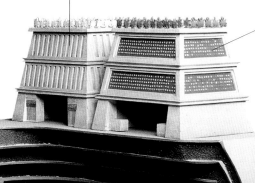

TEMPLE OF HUITZILOPOCHTLI
Huitzilopochtli was the god of war, and also the patron god of the Aztec people.

THE TEMPLE-PYRAMID

Dominating Tenochtitlán's sacred inner city, the Great Pyramid was the Aztecs' most holy site. Twin temples at the top contained the idols of Huitzilopochtli and Tlaloc. Sacrifices took place on a stone outside one of the temples, which was decorated with the skulls of earlier victims. The pyramid was probably about 200 ft (60 m) high and towered above all the buildings around it. Buried beneath it were the remains of at least four earlier pyramids.

Sacrificial stone

This figure is carved in the style of the Toltecs, who ruled Mexico before the Aztecs.

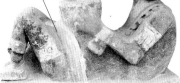

BURYING THE PAST
The Spaniards destroyed the Great Pyramid. But when they built Mexico City on the same site, they accidentally preserved the remains of four temples that lay below.

Chac Mool
This reclining stone figure, called a Chac Mool, was found on the most deeply buried pyramid. The Chac Mool is holding a bowl into which priests may have placed the hearts of their sacrificial victims.

AZTEC WRITING AND COUNTING

I**T WAS EASY TO REMEMBER** dates in Aztec times because they were named after familiar objects, such as animals. Snakes, rabbits, dogs, and eagles all appeared in the calendar. Reading was simple, too: an Aztec codex was full of pictures.

COUNTING

The Aztecs counted in twenties: 1, 20, 400 (20 x 20), and 8,000 (20 x 20 x 20). They showed the numbers in between by repeating each symbol up to 19 times.

Dot and finger signs

Flag sign

Sign for one
The symbol for the number one was a dot or finger. Two dots meant two, and so on, up to 19.

Sign for 20
A flag represented the number 20. Two flags meant 40, and so on, up to 19 flags, or 380.

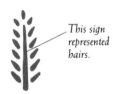
This sign represented hairs.

Sign for a sack of cocoa beans

Sign for 400
The sign for 400 (20 x 20) indicated "as many as there are hairs." It looked like a fir tree.

Sign for 8,000
The symbol for 8,000 (20 x 20 x 20) was a sack of cocoa beans and meant "too many to count."

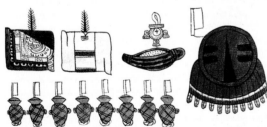

Numbers on a tribute list
This codex picture is part of a tribute list. It demands 400 plain blankets, 400 fancy ones, 8,000 packs of incense, 160 jars of honey, and 20 shields.

Year symbols show the period of the founding of the city.

The founding of Tenochtitlán
On this page from the Codex Mendoza, the large X represents the waters of Lake Texcoco. The figures are Aztec kings, each labeled with his name.

A codex wedding
Spanish priests wrote notes on many codices, explaining what they meant. This scene, from the Codex Mendoza, shows a wedding. The couple is shown with their cloaks knotted together, representing the bond of marriage.

This glyph shows speech.

The footprint glyphs show their route.

Explanation in Spanish

SCRIBES
Trained scribes produced the codex picture-writing, though philosophers (thinkers) and priests could also write.

READING AND WRITING
Aztec writing did not use letters to represent the sounds of speech. Instead, it used pictures and glyphs (symbols). Writing was not supposed to be a complete record; a priest, for example, memorized his people's history, and used a codex to remind him of the details.

Glyph of a smoking shield

Closed eyes indicate death.

A crown shows he is a king.

Smoking Shield
Behind the head of this king is a glyph for his name, which means "smoking shield."

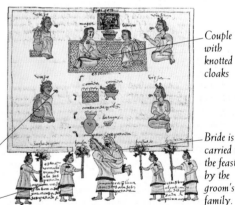
Couple with knotted cloaks

Bride is carried to the feast by the groom's family.

GLYPHS
The simplest writing used pictures of objects. When it was impossible to draw a picture of a word, scribes drew something that readers could link with the word, or something that sounded the same.

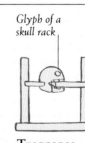

Glyph of a skull rack

Aztecs burned their enemies' temples.

Tochtepec
This province name meant "on rabbit (*tochtli*) hill (*tepetl*)."

Tzonpanco
This place name meant "on (*co*) skull rack (*Tzonpantli*)."

Conquest
A glyph of a burning temple represented the word "conquest."

THE AZTEC CALENDAR

The Aztecs used not one but two calendars. A 365-day calendar showed seasonal events such as harvesting. There were four weeks of five days each in every month. An extra "unlucky" week completed the 18-month year. Religious rituals, though, followed a 260-day calendar that was very different.

On the "13-reed," the fifth sun was created.

This ring shows the 20 days of the month.

The god in the center probably represents the sun or the lord of the earth.

The fifth sun
The sun stone shows Aztec religious beliefs about how the world began and would end. The Aztecs believed that they were living in the time of the fifth (and last) sun. The previous four suns had all died.

The sun stone
This huge stone disk is 12 ft (3.6 m) across. It was discovered on the site of Tenochtitlán's sacred precinct in 1790.

If names and dates were teeth on cogwheels, the same two teeth would meet once every 260 days.

Numbers from 1 to 13

Names of the 20 days

The four square panels around the center show the dates on which the previous four suns perished.

The ritual calendar
Each day had a name and number – both changed daily. The numbers counted from 1 to 13, and the names repeated every 20 days. So if today is one-rabbit, tomorrow will be two-water.

Fire and reeds
This carving of a reed bundle records the "Binding of Years" ceremony. The Aztecs celebrated it once every 52 years when their two calendars coincided.

CARVING OF A REED BUNDLE

Making paper

AZTEC SCRIBES WROTE on strips of paper that were folded to form a codex. These strips, some nearly 40 feet (12 m) long, were created by gluing together sheets of paper made from the bark of fig trees.

The bark of the Ficus benjamina tree was used to make paper.

1 The bark was cut with a sharp stone knife and peeled from the tree. Then it was soaked in running water.

2 The strips of bark were boiled in water and lime. This made the woody fibers softer and easier to separate.

3 The strips were beaten with a ridged stone to merge the fibers into a sheet. The paper toughened as it dried.

4 The paper was trimmed and then polished with a stone. The surface was sealed with white lime.

THE AMERICAS BEFORE THE SPANISH

AFTER THE CONQUEST OF THE Aztecs, the Spaniards gained control of most of Central and South America. The European way of life that they brought with them was sometimes less advanced than the cultures it replaced. The art of these civilizations hints at their richness and variety.

INCAS

The Incas were established in the Andes mountains by AD 1100, but their empire became powerful only in the 15th century. When the Spanish arrived in 1532, Inca control extended from northern Ecuador to the middle of Chile.

Pipes were made from the quills of the condor bird.

Panpipes were – and still are – the most popular instrument in the Andes.

Pots for trade and use
A network of paved roads enabled Inca traders to carry goods like this *Aryballus* jar far from where it was made.

Skilled Inca potters shaped jars without using a wheel.

Handles so that someone could carry the jar on their back.

Music and religion
The Incas used music in their worship of the sun god, especially in the *Inti-raymi* festival on the longest day of the year.

Timeline
This chart shows 25 centuries of civilization in Central and South America. Many of the civilizations ended abruptly in the 16th century, when they were conquered by the Spaniards.

When wealthy Incas died they were buried with gold objects.

This gold feather may have once formed part of a ceremonial headdress.

Gold
The Incas used gold and silver for luxury goods and for ritual objects. They beat the gold into thin sheets with stone hammers, then shaped it and added raised or indented decorations.

MAYA

The Mayan culture reached its peak between AD 300 and 900. Two million Mayan people once lived in 40 cities in and around Mexico's Yucatán peninsula. By the 16th century most of the cities were in ruins.

Jaguar urn
The Maya honored the jaguar as a god of the sun or of the underworld.

Broken pottery or a three-legged pot covered the grave site.

Burial pot
The Maya buried priests and rulers in elaborate underground tombs, but the graves of ordinary people were under the floors of their houses. A pottery urn like this one often formed a child's tomb.

Temple doorway
Mayan cities were ceremonial centers, with spectacular pyramids, temples, and palaces. This carving of a warrior decorated a doorway in the city of Chichén Itzá.

1000 BC	900 BC	800 BC	700 BC	600 BC	500 BC	400 BC	300 BC	200 BC	100 BC	0	AD 100

OLMECS

TEOTIHUACÁN

This ruined city 33 miles (50 km) from Mexico City, is the biggest in ancient America, but we know little about the people who built it. The invading Toltec people wrecked Teotihuacán.

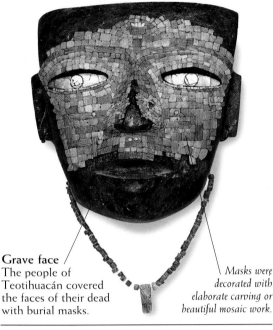

Grave face
The people of Teotihuacán covered the faces of their dead with burial masks.

Masks were decorated with elaborate carving or beautiful mosaic work.

OLMECS

The Olmec people created Central America's earliest civilization on the coast in the south of the Gulf of Mexico. They are famous for carving huge stone heads and for making jade jewelry.

The Olmecs valued jade for its deep green color.

Jade art
Olmec artists created finely detailed jewelry, like this jade necklace.

A human face hangs from a string of jade beads.

TOTONACS

The Totonac people probably migrated from the same homeland as the Aztecs. They lived on the coast of the Gulf of Mexico.

Sun disk
The Totonacs gave the Spaniards this gold sun disk at the command of the Aztec emperor.

MIXTECS

The Mixtecs were flourishing in the Oaxaca region of Mexico by AD 1000. The Aztecs never conquered them.

White spots represent a mouth decoration.

Head man
The Mixtec people made Mexico's best gold jewelry, shown here on a life-size pottery head.

TOLTECS

Much Aztec culture was borrowed from the Toltecs, who controlled central Mexico after the destruction of Teotihuacán. They were the first people in the region to use warfare to expand their empire. At their capital, Tula, the Toltecs built great temple pyramids dedicated to Quetzalcóatl.

A fighter peers from a shell-covered mask.

Military orders
The Toltec's eagle and jaguar regiments inspired Aztec copies. This Toltec ornament shows a coyote warrior.

ZAPOTECS

The Oaxaca valley was the home of the Zapotec people until the expanding Aztec empire drove them into the hills at the end of the 15th century.

Ash urn
Zapotec craftspeople created fine pottery, such as this funeral urn. They also built the beautiful city of Monte Albán.

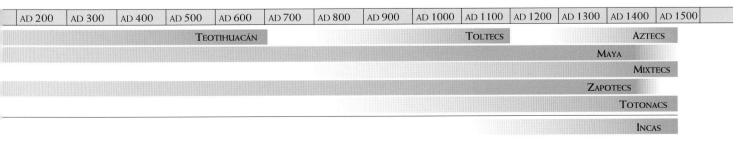

AD 200	AD 300	AD 400	AD 500	AD 600	AD 700	AD 800	AD 900	AD 1000	AD 1100	AD 1200	AD 1300	AD 1400	AD 1500

TEOTIHUACÁN · TOLTECS · AZTECS
MAYA
MIXTECS
ZAPOTECS
TOTONACS
INCAS

Index

Acknowledgments

The publisher would like to thank:
Anna Martin for design assistance;
Sally Hamilton for picture research;
Chris Bernstein for the index; Frances
Berdan for the translation of Aztec
glyphs on p44/45; Michael E. Smith,
Carl L. Martin, and Phil Crossley.

Sources of quotes:
Approximately 200 words from *The
Conquest of New Spain* by Bernal Díaz,
translated by J.M. Cohen (Penguin
Classics, 1963) copyright (c) J.M.
Cohen, 1963. Reproduced by
permission of Penguin Books Ltd.

The History of the Conquest of Mexico by
Francisco Lopez de Gomara,
translated by Lesley Byrd Simpson,
University of California Press, 1964.
*A General History of the Things of New
Spain* by Bernadino de Sahagún, from
translation by Howard F. Cline,
University of Utah Press, 1989, and
from *Cortés and the Downfall of the Aztec
Empire*, John Manchip White, Hamish
Hamilton, 1970.

**The publisher would like to thank
the following for permission to
reproduce their photographs:**
Biblioteca Medicea Laurenziana,
Florence, Italy; Bibliotheque de
l'Assemblée Nationale, Paris, France;
Birmingham City Museum, UK; Bristol
Museum, UK; Cambridge Museum
of Archaeology and Anthropology,
Cambridge, UK; Great Temple
Museum, Mexico City (INAH-CNCA
Mex); London Library; Museo
Nacional de Antropología, Mexico
City; National Museums of Scotland,
UK; Pitt Rivers Museum, Oxford,
UK; Warwick Castle, UK.

Additional photography:
Demetrio Carrasco: 17tr;
Dave King: 47br; **Michel Zabé:** front
jacket bl, 2bl, 2tc, 5, 7tl, 18tl, 37ccl,
37br, 42tc, 42-43b.

Picture Credits
t=top; c=center; b=bottom; l=left;
r=right

**Ancient Art & Architecture
Collection:** 12bl; **The Bodleian
Library, University of Oxford:** Ms
Arch.Seld.A.1.fol.69r: 35br, 36tr,
44cr; **Bridgeman Art Library,
London/New York:** Biblioteca
Nacional, Madrid 29tc, British
Library, London 16bl, 29b,
Giraudon/Museo Nacional de
Historia, Mexico 8bl; **British
Museum, London, UK:** 15tl, 28bl,
31cl; **G. Dagli Orti:** Biblioteca
Nacional, Madrid 6-7, Musée de
l'Amerique 13tr; Musée de la Ville,
Mexico City 9bl, Musée Franz
Mayer, Mexico 40bl, Palazzo Pitti,
Florence 9r, Regional Museum,
Oaxaca 20bc; **Dover Publications,
Inc. New York:** 24tl; **E.T. Archive:**
11cbr, 13cr, 22bl, 25br, 25cc, 28cl,
37tcr, 40br, 42c, 43tr, 43tcl; Private
Collection 12bc, 18-19b, 19tl; **Mary
Evans Picture Library:** 13bl, 14bl;
Werner Forman Archive: British
Museum, London 35tc, Liverpool
Museum, Liverpool 11br, 34cl,
43tcr; **Fotomas Index:** 26-27c;
South American Pictures: Robert
Francis 42bl, Tony Morrison 10cl,
14cl, 31br, 32-33.

Jacket: **Biblioteca Medicea Laurenziana,
Florence, Italy:** front inner flap t;
**Bridgeman Art Library, London/
New York:** front cr; **INAH:** back
inner flap t, back ct; **London Library:**
back tbr; **Michel Zabé:** front bl.